Presented to

_____

On the occasion of

_____

From

_____

Date

_____

Published by Barbour Publishing, Inc., P.O. Box 719, Uhrichsville, Ohio 44683
http://www.barbourbooks.com

Member of the
Evangelical Christian
Publishers Association

Printed in China

A Heart of Purest Gold

A Celebration of a Mother's Love

Compiled by
Ellyn Sanna

BARBOUR
PUBLISHING, INC.

*M*other is
the name for God
in the lips and hearts
of little children.

—WILLIAM MAKEPEACE THACKERAY

As a mother comforts her child,
so will I comfort you.
—*Isaiah 66:13*

*G*od loves us the way a good mother loves—totally, unconditionally, with a nurturing and ever-present care. In fact, as mothers, our love for our children is only a dim reflection of the love God has for His people.

> By this all men will know
> that you are my disciples,
> if you love one another.
> —*John 13:35*

*B*ecause God's love is reflected in ours, our children will learn about God simply through motherhood's love. Oh, we need to teach our children about God and His Word. We need to read them Bible stories and pray with them, answer their questions and take them to church. We need to live in such a way that they'll see what it means to be a Christian. But on much more basic level, they'll understand about a God who always hears, because when they were babies we responded to their cries.

They'll be able to have faith in a God who meets their needs, because we saw that they never went hungry. God's strength and tenderness will be real to them because they caught a glimpse of it in our love, from the time they were born.

So, mothers, never let the world tell you that what you do is not important. Remember, when you rock your babies and sing a lullaby, your arms and voice are God's. When you do load after load of dirty diapers, and then grass-stained play clothes, and finally school clothes smeared with ketchup and chocolate pudding, remember, your hands are God's hands. And when you love your children unconditionally, all the way from colic to adolescent rebellion, you are loving with God's love. Through you, He will imprint Himself on your children's hearts.

The soul can split the sky in two,
And let the face of God shine through.

—EDNA ST. VINCENT MILLAY

*A*s mothers, we can be comforted that not only does God love our children far more than we will ever be able, but He loves us in the same way. We should also be challenged to commit our love for our children to God, to be used by Him as a vehicle to touch our children's lives. This sort of committed love is like a lens that will catch the Spirit's light and magnify it in our children's lives—and as Edna St. Vincent Millay said, this sort of holy love can "split the sky in two," allowing our children to catch a glimpse of God's shining face.

There are two ways of spreading light:
to be the candles or
the mirror that reflects it.

—EDITH WHARTON

Dear God, thank You for Your limitless love. As much as I love my children, I know You love them infinitely more. Please take my flawed, human love for my children and use it for Your glory. Let me be a clear mirror that reflects Your light; help me to magnify You. Amen.

From women's eyes this doctrine
    I derive:
They sparkle still the right
    Promethean fire;
They are the books, the arts,
    the academes,
That show, contain, and nourish
    all the world.

—WILLIAM SHAKESPEARE

Train a child in the way he should go,
and when he is old he will not turn from it.
—*Proverbs 22:6*

*A*s mothers, we have an awesome opportunity: the chance to plant seeds, kindle fires, and impart a legacy of wealth. These seeds may not germinate for many years, sometimes not until after our own death; the fires may only smolder until our children reach adulthood, when suddenly, the Spirit's breath fans them into life. But we can be confident that the things our children learn from us of God and His Son will be a permanent part of their hearts, enriching their lives and eventually their children's lives, an eternal heritage from one generation to the next.

A mother's love!—
How sweet the name!
The holiest, purest, tenderest flame
That kindles from above;
Within a heart of earthly mould
As much of heaven as heart can hold
Nor through eternity grows cold—
That is a mother's love.

—MONTGOMERY

The future destiny of a child is
always the work of its mother.

—NAPOLEON

All that I am or ever hope to be,
I owe to my angel Mother.

— ABRAHAM LINCOLN

All I am I owe to my mother.
I attribute all my success in life to the moral,
intellectual and physical education
I received from her.

—GEORGE WASHINGTON

Who ran to help me when I fell,
And would some pretty story tell,
Or kiss the place to make it well?
My mother.

—ANN TAYLOR

A mother is not a person to lean on,
but a person to make leaning unnecessary.

—DOROTHY CANFIELD FISHER

Sometimes we do not have the chance to love our children from birth—and yet our adopted children and step-children can still find their hearts enriched by the spiritual wealth they receive from us. It is never too late to plant seeds for God, for no matter how late our children come into our lives, God can still touch them through us.

Motherhood

The bravest battle that ever was fought!
Shall I tell you where and when?
On the maps of the world you will find it
not;
'Twas fought by the mothers of men.

Nay not with the cannon of battle-shot,
With a sword or noble pen;
Nay, not with eloquent words or thought
From mouth of wonderful men!

But deep in a walled-up woman's heart—
Of a woman that would not yield,
But bravely, silently bore her part—
Lo, there is the battlefield!

No marshalling troops, no bivouac song,
No banner to gleam and wave;

But oh! those battles, they last so long—
From babyhood to the grave.

Yet, faithful still as a bridge of stars,
She fights in her walled-up town—
Fights on and on in her endless wars,
Then silent, unseen, goes down.

Oh, ye with banners and battle-shot,
And soldiers to shout and praise!
I tell you the kingliest victories fought
Were fought in those silent ways.

O spotless woman in a world of shame,
With splendid and silent scorn,
Go back to God as white as you came—
The Kingliest warrior born!

—JOAQUIN MILLER

Cast all your anxiety on him
because he cares for you.
—*1 Peter 5:7*

*S*ometimes our responsibilities to our children seem too awesome: we must not only keep them clean and safe and healthy, but we must also be responsible for planting spiritual seeds, lighting holy fires, passing along God's wealth. We must take care of them, nurture them, meet their needs—and at the same time we must enable them to grow up strong, dependent on

God rather than ourselves. Sometimes it seems too much to ask of one busy and all too human mother.

Before we start to stumble under this load, though, we need to remember that really, our only responsibility is to God: to be the sort of women He calls us to be. He will take care of the rest. As we live our lives in right relationship with God, His Spirit will be the One who plants the seeds; He will be the One who drops a spark into the tinder of our children's hearts; and He will be the One who uses our consecrated lives to pass along the bounty of His riches.

*H*appy the home when God is there,
And love fills every breast;
When one their wish, and one their prayer,
And one their heavenly rest.

Happy the home where Jesus' Name
Is sweet to every ear;
Where children early speak His fame,
And parents hold Him dear.

—HENRY WARE, JR.

Believe in the Lord Jesus,
and you will be saved—
you and your household.
—*Acts 16:31*

*D*ear Lord, please use me to make my children strong. Teach them of Yourself through me—and may they remember what they learn their whole lives long. You know how many times I fail, You know how selfish and confused I can be sometimes—so use me in spite of myself. And one day in heaven, my children and I will give You all the glory. Amen.

It is not our exalted feelings,
it is our sentiments that build
the necessary home.

—ELIZABETH BOWEN

*O*ur homes are the private spaces that belong uniquely to our own families. They are havens of security that bear the stamp of our personalities—and they are far more than four walls and a roof. What makes a house a home has more to do with our attitude and behaviors—and very little to do with things like curtains and carpets, landscaping and square footage of living space.

Lord, through all generations
you have been our home!
—*Psalm 90:1* (NLT)

*T*he preceding verse from the Ninetieth Psalm indicates what our true home really is: God Himself! The security, pleasure, and comfort that we find in our homes are only one more reflection of God's nature, another way we can catch a glimpse of the God we love. Most of us love our homes—but when we consider that they are actually small reflections of God, then the word "home" takes on even more meaning.

The house is old, the trees are bare,
Moonless above bends twilight's dome;
But what on earth is half so dear,
So longed for, as the hearth of home?

—EMILY BRONTË

Dear Lord, thank You for my home. I ask that You fill it with Your Holy Spirit. Even when I don't have time to polish and dust, may it still shine with Your welcome and love, so that whoever comes in my doors senses that You are present.

Please help me, God, not to fill my home with irritation and frustration; help me not to think that because I'm in the privacy of my own home, I can indulge in uncharitableness. Instead, may my husband and my children and I hand grace back and forth to each other. Amen.

A wife of noble character who can find?
  She is worth far more than rubies.
Her husband has full confidence in her and
  lacks nothing of value.
She brings him good, not harm,
  all the days of her life.
She selects wool and flax and works with eager hands.
She is like the merchant ships,
  bringing her food from afar.
She gets up while it is still dark; she provides food for
  her family and portions for her servant girls.
She considers a field and buys it;
  out of her earnings she plants a vineyard.
She sets about her work vigorously;
  her arms are strong for her tasks.
She sees that her trading is profitable,
  and her lamp does not go out at night.
In her hand she holds the distaff
  and grasps the spindle with her fingers.
She opens her arms to the poor and
  extends her hands to the needy.

When it snows, she has no fear for her household;
    for all of them are clothed in scarlet.
She makes coverings for her bed;
    she is clothed in fine linen and purple.
Her husband is respected at the city gate,
    where he takes his seat among
    the elders of the land.
She makes linen garments and sells them,
    and supplies the merchants with sashes.
She is clothed with strength and dignity;
    she can laugh at the days to come.
She speaks with wisdom,
    and faithful instruction is on her tongue.
She watches over the affairs of her household
    and does not eat the bread of idleness.
Her children arise and call her blessed;
    her husband also, and he praises her:
"Many women do noble things,
    but you surpass them all."
Charm is deceptive, and beauty is fleeting; but a
    woman who fears the LORD is to be praised.

—Proverbs 31:10–30

The Vocation of Maternity

*T*he best convent," I said, "for a woman is the seclusion of her own home. There she may find her vocation and fight her battles, and there she may learn the reality and the earnestness of life."

"Pshaw!" cried she. "Excuse me, however for saying that; but some of the most brilliant girls I know have settled down into mere married women and spend their whole time nursing babies! Think how belittling!"

"Is it more so than spending it dressing, driving, dancing, and the like?"

"Of course it is. I had a friend once who shone like a star in society. She married and had four children as fast as she could. Well! What was the consequence? She lost her beauty, her spirit and animation, lost her youth, and lost her health. The only earthly things she can talk about are teething, dieting, and measles!"

I laughed at this exaggeration. . . . "As you have spoken plainly to me, knowing me to be a wife and mother, you must allow me to speak plainly in return," I began. ". . . You will permit me to say that when you speak contemptuously of the vocation of maternity, you dishonor not only the mother who bore you but the Lord Jesus Himself, who chose to be born of woman and to be ministered unto by her through a helpless infancy."

. . .I thought of my dear ones. . .and I thought of my love for them and theirs for me. And I thought of Him who alone gives reality to even such joys as these.

—from *Stepping Heavenward*
by ELIZABETH PRENTISS

But the fruit of the Spirit is
love, joy, peace, patience, kindness, goodness,
faithfulness, gentleness and self-control.

—*Galatians 5:22-23*

*D*espite our best intentions, all of us have times when life presses down on us so hard that we yield to frustration and anger. Frustration can spring from something as little as a toddler's spilled bowl of Cheerios across our freshly swept kitchen—or an adolescent's rebellion may make frustration grip our throat. We work so hard; after all that we do, when our efforts seem to come to nothing, we too feel like rebelling.

The wise woman builds her house,
but with her own hands
the foolish one tears hers down.
—*Proverbs 14:1*

A gentle answer turns away wrath.
—*Proverbs 15:1*

*D*ear Father, help me to give You everything today: the things I do well—and the things at which I fail. Empower me to accept my circumstances, even life's daily frustrations. Thank You that when I am weak, You are strong. Amen.*

*A*bove all,
love each other deeply,
because love covers over
a multitude of sins.

—1 Peter 4:8

You will find, as you look back upon your life,
that the moments when you have really lived
are the moments when you have
done things in the spirit of love.

—HENRY DRUMMOND

To love abundantly is to live abundantly,
and to love forever is to live forever.

—ANONYMOUS

*B*eing a beautiful woman, a fulfilled woman are not goals we can chase and grab. Instead, our beauty and fulfillment are side-effects that spring from our commitment to Christ. As we live His abundant life, interested in His world and delighting ourselves in all the tiny blessings He sends our way, we will find that we are beautiful and fulfilled simply because we are God's.

*N*o coward soul is mine,
No trembler in the world's
storm-troubled sphere:
I see Heaven's glories shine,
And faith shines equal,
arming me from fear.

—EMILY BRONTË

orrying just seems to come with mother-
hood's territory. It's a bad habit we all fall into. As
Emily Brontë's poem says, the only solution is to
keep our eyes fixed on "Heaven's glories" rather than
the "world's storm-troubled sphere." Faith is our
only shield against fear and worry.

> She never quite leaves her children at home,
> even when she doesn't take them along.

—MARGARET CULKIN BANNING

*S*ometimes we feel weighted down with the burden of seeing to our children's health and safety. The world is full of dangers that threaten our children's lives—and we yield to the false thinking that says only we, their mothers, can keep them safe. We know that our children's needs must come first, and so we feel we must give up every other ministry or profession, and devote ourselves totally to their well-being.

We forget that both we and our children are in God's hands. We can never protect our children from every danger, for only God can truly see to their well-being—and when we put ourselves in His hands, He can balance our motherhood with our other occupations.

And all thy children shall be taught of the Lord;
and great shall be the peace of thy children.
—*Isaiah 54:13* (KJV)

*T*hank You, Father, for being not only my Father but my children's. When I am scared and worried for their safety and well-being, help me to trust them each to You, knowing that You love them far more than I am capable. Thank You that You will always watch them, even when I cannot. I know they can never go so far from home that they will be lost to Your love.

*B*e thou my Vision,
O Lord of my heart;
Nought be all else to me,
Save that Thou art.

—MARY BYRNE

Through all of motherhood's joys and sorrows, fulfillment and frustration, we have a companion who never leaves us, whether we sense His presence or not. He smiles and laughs with us; He cries with us and understands our frustrations. In every aspect of a mother's heart, we find images of this holy companion. He never leaves us.

Dear God,
You know how much
I love my family.
Help me to remember that
when I express my love to them,
I am also loving You.
Remind me to live my life
in love's service.
Please bring me back when I stray
out of this "royal way."
I love You, Father.
Give me strength
to love You more.

Amen.